Contents

18

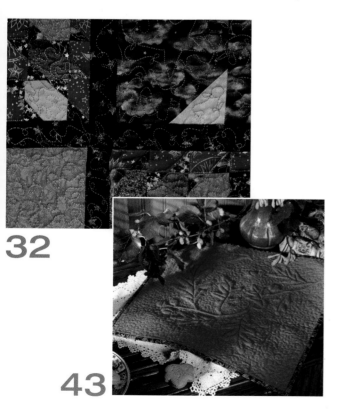

32

43

From the Staff

Whether you're a seasoned hand quilter or a beginner who's always wanted to learn to hand-quilt, this one-stop, quilter-tested reference guide will show you everything you need to know about this time-honored technique.

In *Teach Yourself to Hand-Quilt*, we've included information about all the basic supplies you'll need (*pages 2–14*). You'll also find step-by-step how-tos, a gallery of inspiring quilting patterns to peruse (*pages 27–35*), and loads of useful tips and ideas scattered throughout—all aimed at making quilting easier and more fun for you. And to showcase your refreshed or newly acquired skills, try your hand at one or both of the featured tabletop-size projects (*pages 36–47*).

We hope you'll enjoy this guide, that you'll refer to it often over the years, and that it will help make your hand quilting even more satisfying.

Happy Quilting!

A Look at the Supplies

QUILTING SUPPLIES CAN BE AS BASIC as scissors, needle, and thread, or more complex with specialty tools designed for a specific purpose. There are hundreds of items available to make quilting tasks easier, more accurate, and more fun. Whether you're a gadget-lover or a minimalist, knowing what the tools are, what to use them for, and why they're useful is essential.

Marking Tools

Many products are available for marking sewing lines and quilting designs on a quilt top. Useful supplies include fabric markers, templates, and pattern guides.

Variances in fabric contrast (light to dark) and fabric quality make marking different for each project. A variety of markers may be needed for a single project. Before you begin to mark your quilt top, try the markers on fabric scraps and wash the scraps as you will the quilt to be sure the marks will wash out.

Templates and pattern guides will vary according to the needs of each project.

FABRIC MARKERS

Artist's pencil: This silver pencil often works on both light and dark fabrics.

Chalk pencil: The chalk tends to brush away, so it is best to mark as you go with this pencil.

Mechanical pencil: Use hard lead (0.5) and mark lightly so that stitching or quilting will cover it.

Pounce: This is chalk in a bag. Pounce or pat the bag on a stencil, leaving a chalk design on the fabric. The chalk disappears easily, so mark as you go.

Soap sliver: Sharpen the edges of a leftover soap bar for a marker that washes out easily.

Soapstone marker: If kept sharp, this marker will show up on light and dark fabrics.

Wash-out graphite marker: Keep the sharpener handy for this marker that works well on light and dark fabrics.

Wash-out pen or pencil: These markers maintain a point and are easy to see. Refer to the manufacturer's instructions to remove the markings, and test them on scraps of your fabric to make sure the marks will wash out. *Note: Humidity may make the marks disappear, and applying heat to them may make them permanent.*

TEMPLATES AND PATTERN GUIDES

A template is a pattern made from extra-sturdy material so you can trace around it many times without wearing away the edges.

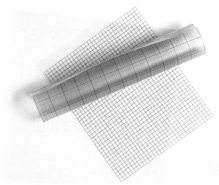

Quilting stencils and templates: Precut stencils and templates in a variety of shapes and sizes are available from quilt shops. These may be made from template plastic or a heavier-weight acrylic plastic. They can be traced around multiple times without wearing away any edges.

Some quilting stencils also are made from paper. They are designed to be stitched through and torn away after the design is completed.

Template plastic: Template plastic is an easy-to-cut, translucent material available at quilt shops and crafts supply stores.

Its translucency allows you to trace a pattern directly onto its surface with pencil or permanent marker to make a stencil or template.

TIP
When using any marking tool, keep the point sharp to get a fine yet visible line.

Test a variety of materials as some are heat-resistant (helpful when ironing over template edges) and some are not. Other varieties are gridded for accuracy in tracing or shaded for better visibility.

Freezer paper: Available at quilt shops and supermarkets, freezer paper allows you to create an iron-on template. Trace a shape onto the dull side of the freezer paper, cut it out, and press it directly onto the fabric with an iron.

Graph-paper: Use the printed lines on graph paper to draw a pattern piece. Glue the graph-paper pattern to template plastic, tag board, or cardboard. Allow the adhesive to dry before cutting through all layers at once to make an accurate template.

Clear vinyl: Also known as upholstery vinyl, this material is used by hand quilters to make overlays for accurately positioning appliqué pieces on foundation fabric.

Tape: Several types of tape are used to mark quilting and stitching lines—quilter's tape, painter's tape, paper tape, and masking tape are common choices. Quilter's tape is exactly ¼" wide; place it at the edge of your fabric and stitch alongside it for a ¼" seam allowance.

Specialty tapes in widths from ¹⁄₁₆" to 1" and wider are preprinted with lines to aid quilters in evenly spacing hand quilting or decorative stitches, such as a blanket stitch.

Some quilters use masking tape as a guide for straight-line machine or hand quilting. *Note: Do not leave masking tape on fabric for an extended period of time as the adhesive from the tape may leave a residue. Painter's tape is less sticky than masking tape and also can be used as a guide for straight-line quilting.*

Quilting requires a good pair of scissors. Most quilters use several pairs, each designed for a different purpose. Choose your cutting tools with care, making certain they are of the highest quality you can afford. It's better to have two or three sharp pairs of scissors than a drawer full of seldom-used, dull pairs.

Choose your scissors and shears from the following.

Thread clippers (A): Use for cutting threads. A single style is used by both left- and right-handed persons.

Craft scissors and knife-edge straight trimmers (B): Left- and right-handed styles are available.

Embroidery scissors (C): Use for thread cutting. Left- and right-handed styles are available.

Appliqué scissors (D): Use for close trimming; a special duckbill protects underneath layers of fabric. Left- and right-handed styles are available.

Knife-edge bent trimmers or shears (E): Use for general cutting and sewing. The bent handle and flat edge provide accuracy when cutting on a flat surface. Left- and right-handed styles are available.

Spring-action scissors (F): Small and large sizes are available. Ideal for use by persons with weakened hands or for lengthy cutting sessions. A single style is used by both left- and right-handed persons.

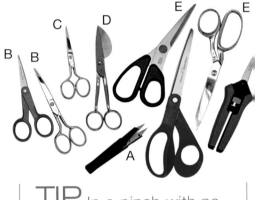

TIP In a pinch with no scissors in sight? Use nail clippers to cut your thread.

Can't see the lines of your ruler on the fabric? When working with dark fabrics, choose a ruler with yellow or white markings. For light fabrics, choose one with black markings.

Thread & Needles

Thread and needles are at the heart of quilting as the two elements that literally hold everything together. Choosing the right type and size of needle and thread can make a big difference in the success of your quilting project. Follow three general guidelines: Match the thread type to the fabric fiber content, select the needle type based on the fabric being used, and select the needle size to match the thread.

THREAD

Thread has multiple roles, from holding together patchwork to anchoring the fabric to the batting. Thread also plays a role in decoration, adding color, design, and texture to the quilt surface.

For piecing and most quilting, it's best to match the thread fiber to the fabric. Since most quilters use cotton fabric, 100 percent cotton thread is the best thread choice. Cotton thread is equal in strength to cotton fabric and should wear evenly. Synthetic threads, such as polyester, rayon, and nylon, are quite strong and can wear cotton fibers at the seams. For decorative quilting or embellishing, threads other than cotton may be appropriate. Be sure your thread choice is suitable for the task; thread made for hand quilting, such as glazed cotton thread, should not be used in your sewing machine.

Thread Types

100 PERCENT COTTON

Cotton thread is a staple in quilting. This thread works well with cotton fabric and is strong enough to create pieces that are durable. Hundreds of color choices are available in a variety of weights, although not all weights are created equal. Most cotton threads are two- or three-ply.

COTTON-WRAPPED POLYESTER

Wrapping cotton around a polyester core creates a stronger thread with the finish characteristics of cotton thread. This thread is best used with fabric blends because it

TIP The fabric strength should be greater than that of the thread used for piecing. If seams are stressed, thread will give way before the fabric tears. For this reason, strong polyester thread should not be used for piecing cotton fabrics.

provides a little stretch. It's important to use a needle with a large eye to prevent stripping the cotton wrap from the polyester core.

METALLIC

The sheen and variety of colors available make metallic threads appealing for decorative stitching. However, metallic threads have a tendency to fray and break more often than cotton thread.

PERLE COTTON

Soft and yarnlike, perle cotton is used for needlework projects or quilt embellishment. Typical weights used in quilting include Nos. 3, 5, 8, and 12. The higher the number, the finer the thread.

POLYESTER

This thread is designed for sewing with knits because the filament has the same stretch as knit fabric. Polyester thread should not be used with cotton fabrics for piecing or quilting because it can be abrasive to soft cotton fibers and cause the fabric to tear at the seams.

RAYON

The soft, lustrous characteristics of rayon thread and the hundreds of colors available make it ideal for embellishment. It's often used for decorative quilting or embroidery. This thread is not strong enough and doesn't wear well enough to be used in piecing a quilt and should be alternated with a cotton thread when quilting a project that will get lots of wear.

Typical thread weights are 30, 40, 50, 60, and 80. If the number of plies is equal, the higher number indicates finer thread. For example, a 50-weight three-ply thread is finer than a 40-weight three-ply thread.

SILK

Silk thread is stronger than cotton because it is a continuous filament, unlike cotton's short spun fibers. Silk also has more stretch than cotton thread. Some quilters prefer to use silk thread for hand appliqué because it glides through the fabric more easily than cotton and is usually finer, making it easier to hide the stitches. It also is less prone to fraying, allowing a longer length of thread to be used.

VARIEGATED

This term applies to thread in which the color changes back and forth from light to dark throughout the strand or revolves through a range of colors to create a rainbow effect. It is available in both cotton and rayon.

WATER-SOLUBLE

This thread dissolves in water. Use it to baste a quilt or anchor trapunto or reverse appliqué. Once the project is completed, immerse it in water to dissolve the thread.

Be sure to store the thread in a dry, humidity-controlled location.

HAND-QUILTING NEEDLES

Make your hand sewing easier by selecting the right needle. Myriad hand-sewing needles are available through quilt shops and fabric stores. Understanding the type, size, and uses of each needle will help you select the one most suitable for your project. Also note that it is important to change needles frequently as they become dull with use.

Hand- and machine-sewing needles have some similarities, but be aware that once you've mastered the numbers for hand-sewing needles, you'll need to learn a whole new set for machine-needle sizes.

CHOOSING A THREAD COLOR

Match thread and fabric colors when you want the quilting design to blend in with the quilt top or backing, such as when stippling or quilting in the ditch. When you want to accentuate the quilting, choose a thread color in contrast to the fabric color. This may be especially important when using decorative threads as a strong design element.

Hand Needle Sizes

A hand needle's size is determined by its diameter. There are two ranges in diameter size: 1 to 15 and 13 to 28. The diameter of a specific size remains consistent across the various needle types. In each case, the larger the number, the finer the needle; all size 12 needles are finer than size 8, for example.

Troubleshooting Checklist for Thread Breakage

If you're having trouble with thread breaking, check these possible causes.

● **Damaged or incorrect needle:** Change the needle as it may be dull from overuse or have a burr or nick. If the needle is new, make sure it is the correct size and the eye is large enough for the thread type and weight being used (see chart on *page 8*).

● **Defective or old thread:** Lower-quality threads may have thick and thin spots that lead to breakage. Thread that is too old becomes brittle as it ages, causing it to break easily.

● **Operator error:** Pushing or pulling on the fabric or allowing drag to be created by hanging a heavy quilt over your work surface can increase stress on the thread and cause breakage.

● **Wrong thread:** You may have the wrong thread for your fabric. Change the thread, and quilt a fabric scrap to see how a different thread performs.

TIP Thread marked 50/3 (50-weight and three-ply) works for both hand and machine quilting on cotton fabric. It's considered a medium-weight thread.

Hand Needle Points

Hand-quilting needles have a sharp point that pierces fabric readily. Working with a dull needle can be frustrating and produce less desirable results. Just as with machine sewing, switching to a new needle after several hours of sewing is optimal.

Hand Needle Eyes

Needles with small, round eyes carry fine thread (approximately equal in diameter to the needle itself) that slides easily through the fabric. Longer needle eyes accommodate thicker threads and yarns. The oval eye found in tapestry and chenille needles helps create an opening in the fabric for thick, sometimes coarse fibers to pass through. Use the smallest needle appropriate to the thread to minimize holes in your fabric.

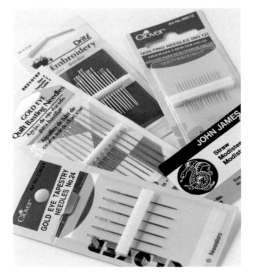

Hand Needle Types

Quilters have many different uses for hand-sewing needles—hand piecing, hand quilting, appliqué, embroidery, tying, and securing binding. The point of the needle, the shape of the eye, and the needle's length in proportion to the eye determine its type.

Short needles are easier to maneuver in small spaces. For tasks that require long stitches or lots of stitches on the needle, like basting, weaving, and gathering, there are longer needles.

Betweens have a small, round eye and come in sizes 4 to 12. Betweens are short and made of fine wire, resulting in a strong, flexible needle that's ideal for hand quilting, appliqué, and sewing binding.

This is the most commonly used needle for hand quilting.

If you experience problems with breaking or twisting thread, the cause may be a needle mismatched to the thread type.

For hand-sewing needles, the larger the number, the smaller or finer the needle.

Sharps have a small, round eye and come in sizes 4 to 12. They are used for hand piecing, appliqué, general sewing, embroidery work that uses fine threads, and sewing binding.

Straw, or milliners, needles come in sizes 4 to 10. They have a small, round eye and are very long. These needles are often used for basting, gathering, and appliqué.

Beading needles are extra long with long, narrow eyes. Available in sizes 10 to 15, these needles are used for embellishment, beading, and sequin work.

Chenille needles have a long, oval eye and come in sizes 12 to 26. A chenille needle is often used for heavyweight thread, embroidery, and tying quilts.

Darners have a long, narrow eye. This needle type comes in sizes 1 to 11 and is used for basting, weaving, and tying quilts. Darners are also available in finer sizes ranging from 14 to 18. Long darners (double-long needles) come in sizes 1 to 15 and can be used for weaving or tying quilts.

Embroidery needles come in sizes 1 to 10 and have a long, narrow eye. They are most often used for embroidery work with thicker decorative thread and wool thread.

Troubleshooting Checklist for Needles

Your needle may be the culprit if these problems crop up while you're hand-quilting.

● **Bearding** refers to the little white dots you see where your stitches are made. It occurs when batting comes through your fabric. Often the problem is caused by using too large a needle, a dull needle, or a needle that has a burr or nick.

● **Thread shredding** occurs for several reasons. The needle eye may be too small for the thread weight. If you have difficulty pulling the thread through the needle with ease, choose a needle with a larger eye. If you're hand-quilting, you may have begun with a length of thread that's too long. If so, the thread may have become worn from being pulled through the fabric and batting too many times. If you're working with a metallic thread, be sure to use a metallic needle specifically designed to diminish thread shredding.

HAND-SEWING NEEDLES

SMALL ROUND EYES	TYPE	LENGTH / DIAMETER	SIZES	USES
#8 Sharps	SHARPS	Medium / 41–76 mm	4–12	Hand piecing; general sewing; fine thread embroidery; sewing binding
#8 Betweens	BETWEENS/ QUILTING	Short / 41–76 mm	4–12	Hand piecing and quilting; appliqué; sewing binding
#9 Straw	STRAW/ MILLINERS	Long / 53–76 mm	4–10	Basting; gathering; appliqué
#8 Glovers	GLOVERS	Medium with a triangular point / 86–102 mm	1–3	Leather
		53–76 mm	4–10	Leather

LONG NARROW EYES

	TYPE	LENGTH / DIAMETER	SIZES	USES
#8 Embroidery	EMBROIDERY	Medium / 53–102 mm	1–10	Wool thread embroidery
#9 Darners	DARNERS	Long / 46–102 mm	1–11	Basting; weaving; tying comforters
		127–234 mm	14–18	
#9 Long Darners	LONG DARNERS	Double long / 61–183 mm	1–15	Weaving; tying comforters
#10 Beading	BEADING	Double long / 25–46 mm	10–15	Bead and sequin work

LONG OVAL EYES

	TYPE	LENGTH / DIAMETER	SIZES	USES
#26 Chenille	CHENILLE	Medium / 61–234 mm	12–26	Heavy thread embroidery; tying comforters
#26 Tapestry	TAPESTRY/ CROSS-STITCH	Medium with blunt point / 46–234 mm	13–28	Needlepoint; cross-stitch

TIP Before working on your project, do a test to see how the thread-and-needle combination works. Sew together long strips of fabric to test piecing, or appliqué a patch. Create a little quilt sandwich (top, batting, and backing) and evaluate your quilting stitches.

Your Work Space

Although quilting may seem like a sedentary activity, it takes energy, and the repetitive actions can stress joints and muscles. To keep quilting comfortably, follow a few simple tips for posture and position.

POSTURE

Be aware of your body posture. A straight back with your head and neck aligned and feet flat on the floor gives you the most support. Sitting or working at awkward angles and performing repetitive motions create situations that can cause injuries.

90 DEGREES

Keep this angle in mind whenever you sit down to perform a task.

Your back and legs should be at a 90° angle. Your upper and lower legs should form a 90° angle at your knees. When your feet are flat on the floor, your ankles also will be at a 90° angle.

Next, look at your arms. Your elbows should be at a 90° angle with your forearms parallel to the work surface. Keep your elbows close to your sides and your shoulders straight.

TABLE OR LARGE WORK SURFACE

A large work surface allows you to lay out long yardages of fabric when cutting or to handle a medium- to large-size quilt for basting.

ADJUST THE WORK SURFACE

Once you have determined your 90° positions, raise or lower your work surface and/or chair in order to hold these positions and work comfortably.

If you raise your chair so your arms are at the work surface, you may not be able to keep your feet flat on the floor. Put a sturdy box or

platform step under your feet so your knees and ankles stay at their 90° angles.

Give yourself time. If you have been working at awkward angles, your body may have adapted and it may feel strange when you adjust your posture. Stay with the correct posture and you will benefit in the long run.

Align your cutting surface to hip height to eliminate the need to bend over and unnecessarily put strain on your back and shoulder muscles.

If you're rotary-cutting, use sharp rotary blades and rulers with nonskid material to decrease the amount of pressure needed to cut fabric, thus reducing the strain on your body.

When hand-quilting with a frame, it is best to first position your chair with your body at 90° angles. Next, measure the distance between your elbows (bent at 90°) and the floor. Set the front roller bar of the quilting frame at this height, then adjust the back of the quilting frame.

DESIGN WALL

Having a vertical surface on which to lay out fabric choices can help you visualize how they might look in a quilt.

For a permanent or portable design wall, cover foam core or board insulation with a napped material, such as felt or flannel, that will hold small fabric pieces in place. Some designers use the flannel backing of a vinyl tablecloth, which can be rolled up between projects or hung on a hanger.

LIGHTING

Quilting requires overall lighting and nonglare directional lighting to avoid eyestrain and produce high-quality results. Review your quilting areas for lighting, and invest in the appropriate fixtures to eliminate the headaches and vision problems that can result from eyestrain.

Several specialty lamps and bulbs specifically designed for quilters are available at quilt shops. Some are designed to more accurately reflect fabric colors, filtering out excess yellow and blue tones that household bulbs can cast. These can be especially helpful when you are selecting fabric combinations for your quilts and if your quilting area does not have abundant natural daylight.

KEEP MOVING FOR PERSONAL COMFORT

Though it's easy to get lost in your quilting, it is important to your overall health to pause for a few minutes every hour to step away from your quilting frame and stretch. If you take time to reposition yourself periodically, you can reduce muscle fatigue and eyestrain and enjoy several hours of quilting.

Speak with your health care provider about specific exercises that can help strengthen your neck, back, shoulders, arms, wrists, and hands.

Checklist for Healthy Quilting

- Avoid reaching up to the work surface.
- Sit up straight.
- Avoid reaching over or out to the work surface (keep elbows at your side).
- Take 10-minute breaks every hour.
- Drink extra water.

General Tools & Supplies

Beyond the all-important needle and thread choices that hand quilters make, there are a few other tools required. Personal preference dictates the use of many of the optional accessories.

ADHESIVES

BASTING SPRAY

Many brands of basting spray are available. The main point of difference is the ability to reposition the fabric. The sprays are often a good option for temporarily holding appliqués in place or for basting a small quilt or wall hanging together. Follow label directions and work in a ventilated area.

FABRIC GLUE

Fabric glue comes in several different forms. Whether you choose a type that comes in a bottle with a needle-tip applicator or a glue-stick version, make certain it is designed for use with fabric and is water-soluble and acid-free. When dry, fabric glue is more pliable than standard glue, and often its temporary bond allows you to reposition pieces without leaving permanent residue on your quilt.

FUSIBLE WEB

Available in prepackaged sheets or rolls, by the yard off the bolt, or as a narrow-width tape, fusible web is an iron-on adhesive that in nearly every case creates a permanent bond between layers of fabric.

Fusible web has adhesive on both sides with a paper backing on one of the sides. It is most often used for machine appliqué. The standard version for quilting is a lightweight, paper-backed fusible web specifically designed to be stitched through. When purchasing this product, check the label to make sure you've selected a sew-through type. If you are certain that you will not be sewing through the fused fabric (e.g., unfinished appliqué edges), you may wish to use a heavyweight, no-sew fusible web.

The manufacturer's instructions for adhering fusible web vary by brand. Follow the instructions that come with your fusible web to ensure that you're using the correct iron temperature setting and know whether to use a dry or steam iron. These factors, along with the length of time you press, are critical to attaining a secure bond between the fusible web and the fabric.

BATTING

The material that goes between the quilt top and backing—batting—can vary from quilt to quilt. Learn the characteristics and properties of batting for the ideal match (see page 13 for complete information).

MEASURING TAPES

A measuring tape is essential for large measurements, such as border lengths or squaring up quilts. Make sure to purchase one that is long enough to cover your largest quilt measurement so you don't have to move the tape midway. Be aware that over time, a well-used cloth measuring tape may stretch and thus become inaccurate.

NEEDLE THREADERS

This device makes getting the thread through the needle eye easier. Try several models to see which works best for your vision and coordination skills. Keep one close at hand to prevent eyestrain.

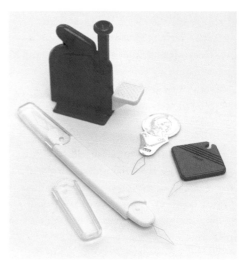

PINCUSHIONS

Pincushions are available in numerous styles, from the standard tomato shape so many of us are familiar with to wrist, magnetic tabletop, and even decorative ones. Select a style that's easy for you to use.

The strawberry-shape, emery-filled needle cushion that is often attached to a tomato-shape pincushion is an important aid in keeping your needles sharp and tarnish-free. Run all hand-sewing needles through the emery cushion before using them to remove any slight burrs, nicks, or residue.

PINS

Experiment with different pins, shown *below, left to right,* to determine which ones work best for your needs.

Glass-head pins allow you to press fabric pieces with pins in place without melting the pins' heads.

Appliqué pins range from ¾" to 1¼" in length. They are designed to securely hold work in place yet prevent the sewing thread from getting snagged with each stitch.

Flat flower pins have heads shaped like flowers. The long shaft makes them easy to grab and helps the pins stay put in the fabric.

Extra-fine, or silk, pins have thin shafts and sharp points. These pins make a small hole and are easy to insert.

Safety pins (not shown) are clasps with a guard covering the point when closed. Use safety pins that are at least 1" long to pin-baste a quilt.

Choose stainless-steel pins that are rust-proof and will not tarnish.

There are several devices, including a spoon, that can be used to help close the pins, preventing hand fatigue. In addition, there are curved basting safety pins that slide in place without moving the quilt sandwich.

QUILTING FRAMES AND HOOPS

Quilting hoops, which generally are sturdier than embroidery hoops, may be round, oval, square, or rectangular. Semicircular hoops, which are good for stitching borders or other areas close to a quilt's edges, are also available.

Hoops come in all sizes, but one with a diameter of 10" to 20" should be able to accommodate most quilting needs.

Some hoops have a detachable floor stand that frees your hands for stitching and permits the hoop to be tilted and/or raised.

Most quilting frames consist of wooden top rails in a rectangular shape supported by sturdy legs. They come in a wide range of sizes (30" to 120") so they can handle quilts up to king size.

When using a frame, a quilt's edges are pinned or stitched flat to the rails so the layers are smooth, straight, and secure. One or both pairs of frame rails can be rotated to roll up the quilt and facilitate working on a small area at a time.

A quilt frame must remain set up and in place until the quilting is complete.

SEAM RIPPERS

Although quilters don't enjoy "reverse sewing," sometimes it is necessary to remove a line of stitching. A sharp, good-quality seam ripper can make the task of removing stitches easy and cause the least damage possible to your fabric.

THIMBLES

Protect your fingers while quilting with a variety of thimbles. Choose from metal or

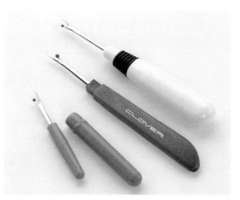

leather, or consider special pads that stick to your fingers. Try them all to determine the style that works best for you. For difficult-to-fit fingers or simply increased comfort, custom-made thimbles are widely available.

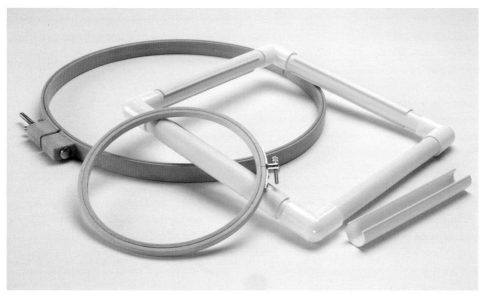

Batting Choices

The soft layer of material that goes between the quilt top and backing—the batting—gives a quilt dimension and definition and offers warmth. Because the best batting to use can vary from quilt to quilt, it is wise to learn the characteristics and properties of batting for the ideal match.

Your beautiful quilt top deserves a batting and backing that will enhance the finished project and be suited to its use. Historically, quiltmakers used whatever natural fibers were on hand for the quilt's middle layer or batting, but today's quilters can choose from natural and synthetic products that have a variety of characteristics.

Because batting comes in various thicknesses and fibers, it can make a quilt flat or puffy, stiff or drapable. It is available by the yard or packaged to fit standard bed sizes.

The batting you use should complement the nature and use of your finished quilt. Check package labels, talk to other quilters, and test samples to find the batting with the qualities that are important for your project.

BATTING QUALITIES

Carefully read the manufacturer's label to learn the specific qualities of a particular batting.

Bearding

Some battings beard, or have fibers migrate through the quilt top, more than others, but any bearding is a problem when light battings are used with dark fabrics, or the reverse. Test battings with your quilt's fabrics to see if bearding will be a problem. Make sure you're not using an untreated batting. Though bearding can be attributed to a problem with your batting choice, it also could be caused by a very loosely woven fabric. Knowing what qualities to watch for can make a significant difference in your satisfaction with the finished quilt.

TIP Try black batting. It is difficult to avoid bearding when quilting large areas of black fabrics. If you're working on a dark color quilt, you may wish to consider a black batting.

Drapability

The density or sparseness of the quilting and the loft of the batting will affect the drape, or relative stiffness or softness, of the finished quilt. In general, a thinner batting and more dense quilting will result in a quilt with a softer drape. A thicker batting in a quilt that has been tied, rather than heavily quilted, will have less drape.

Grain Line

Battings can have a grain line just as fabric does. The lengthwise grain is stable and doesn't have much give, while the crosswise grain will be stretchy. In order to prevent unwanted distortion, match the batting's lengthwise grain with the backing fabric's lengthwise grain. Quilt the lengthwise grain first to limit distortion.

Loft

The thickness of a batting is referred to as its loft. Differing loft levels result in differing appearances in a finished quilt. Refer to the chart, *opposite,* to choose a loft compatible with your finishing method. Keep in mind that the higher the loft, the less drapability in the finished quilt.

Resiliency

Resiliency refers to the batting's ability to regain its original shape. A resilient batting, such as one made from polyester, will spring back when unfolded and resist creasing. This may be a desirable feature if you want a finished quilt with a puffy appearance. Cotton battings are less resilient and more prone to creasing, but some of their other qualities may compensate and make their use desirable. A cotton/polyester blend batting is somewhere in between in terms of resilience.

Warmth

Cotton battings have the ability to absorb moisture, thus offering cooling comfort in the summer and a natural warmth in the winter. Wool battings provide warmth with little weight. Synthetic fibers, such as polyester, lack the breathability of natural fibers.

Washability and Shrinkage

Although polyester and wool battings resist shrinkage, cotton battings can shrink from 3 percent to 5 percent.

Check the package label, then decide whether or not to preshrink a batting. Some quilters prefer the puckered, antique look that comes from a batting that shrinks after it's been quilted.

SELECT YOUR BATTING

Choose a batting based on the finished quilt's intended use and desired appearance.

Quilting Distance

The distance between quilting stitches is largely determined by batting qualities. The manufacturer's label will specify the maximum distance between stitching rows. If you exceed the recommended maximum distance, your batting will shift and bunch up later.

GENERAL BATTING CHARACTERISTICS

Batting Type	Advantages	Disadvantages	Characteristics
100 Percent Cotton	Natural fiber so batting breathes. Resists fiber migration. Readily available.	May have seeds and plant residue that can release oils and stain the quilt. Often cannot be prewashed. Shrinks 3 percent to 5 percent when washed. May be too dense for beginning hand quilters.	Can give a puckered appearance if washed after quilted. Soft, drapable. Good for experienced quilter's fine hand-quilting stitches or machine quilting.
Cotton/Polyester Blends 80/20 50/50	Some natural fibers so batting breathes. Resists fiber migration. Easy for beginning hand quilters to needle. Readily available.	Some shrinkage, which can be avoided in many cases, if desired, by prewashing.	Low to medium loft. Drapable. Good for hand quilting and machine quilting.
Wool and Wool Blends	Natural insulator. Preshrunk. Available in black.	May have inconsistent loft. May need to be encased in cheesecloth or scrim if not bonded.	Blend of fibers from different animal breeds. Resiliency enhances quilting stitches. Soft, drapable. Good for hand and machine quilting.
Silk	Good choice for quilted garments. Does not shrink. Can be washed.	Expensive. Not widely available. Damaged by exposure to direct sunlight.	Has excellent body and drape. Lightweight. Good for machine quilting.
Flannel	Lightweight alternative to traditional batting. Readily available.	Extreme low loft limits quilting pattern development.	100 percent cotton. Lightweight, thin. Good for machine quilting.
Polyester	Resilient, lightweight. Cannot be harmed by moths or mildew. Readily available. Available in black.	Synthetic fibers lack breathability.	Available in many lofts. Suitable for hand quilting and machine quilting. High loft is good for tied quilts and comforters.
Fusible	No need to prewash. Eliminates need for basting. Good choice for small projects.	Limited batting options and sizes. Adds adhesive to quilt. Difficult for hand quilters to needle.	Good for machine quilting. Eliminates need for basting.

If you know you want to tie your finished quilt project, it is essential that to select a quilt batting that allows a wide distance between stitches. A heavily quilted design will require a different choice of batting. Always refer to the package label to see if the batting you're considering is compatible with the amount of quilting you plan to do on your project.

Intended Use
Consider the intended use of your quilt. Is it a baby quilt that will be washed and dried extensively? Will it be placed on a child's bed and get pulled and tugged? Are you making a wall hanging that needs to maintain sharp, crisp corners? Or are you making a quilt that you want to drape loosely over a bed and tuck beneath the pillows? Is it an heirloom project that will be used sparingly and only laundered once every few years? Or is it a decorative item that will never be washed? Is it a table runner that needs to lie extremely flat? Questions such as these will help you evaluate which batting is best for your project.

Desired Appearance
Consider the fabrics in the quilt top and the backing. Are they light or dark colors? If you select a dark batting, will it show through the fabric? Would a white batting beard through the top?

Did you wash and dry your fabrics before making your quilt top, or do you want the layers to shrink as one after you've finished the project to result in an antique appearance?

What loft do you want your quilt to have? Do you want it to be big and puffy or flat and drapable?

Quilting Method
Do you plan to quilt your project by hand or machine, or are you tying it? Do you want to use perle cotton and a utility stitch to create a folk art look?

The batting type dictates the spacing between rows of quilting, so determine whether you want dense or sparse stitching before selecting a batting. The manufacturer's label will specify the maximum distance. If you exceed this distance when quilting, your batting will shift and bunch up, causing your

finished project to look uneven. If you want to tie a project, select a batting that specifies a wide distance between stitches.

Fibers
Consider whether you want natural, synthetic, or a blend of fibers. Each has different qualities. (For more information, see the General Batting Characteristics chart on *page 13*.)

Size
The quilt batting needs to be larger than the quilt top to allow for take-up during quilting and for stabilization when using a quilting frame. Add 6" to both the length and width measurements to allow an extra 3" of batting around the entire quilt.

Testing
To be sure that you'll be satisfied with your choice of batting, test it with similar fabrics, thread, quilting technique, and washing process (if desired) used in the quilt top.

Since same-type battings from different manufacturers can vary in qualities and results, keep records of the battings you use. Your personal preferences will help you make future selections.

In addition, when looking at other quilters' finished projects, ask the makers what battings they used. The answers can help you determine the finished appearance you prefer.

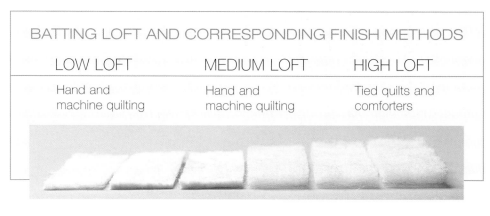

BATTING LOFT AND CORRESPONDING FINISH METHODS

LOW LOFT	MEDIUM LOFT	HIGH LOFT
Hand and machine quilting	Hand and machine quilting	Tied quilts and comforters

TIP **Is it possible to join two pieces of batting?**
If your batting is too small, you can join two batting pieces to make the necessary size. Follow this process to prevent a seam line ridge where the pieces join. Overlap the batting pieces by several inches. Rotary-cut a rolling curve through the overlapped area. Remove the excess and butt the curved edges together. Use a herringbone stitch, *right,* to join the two pieces.

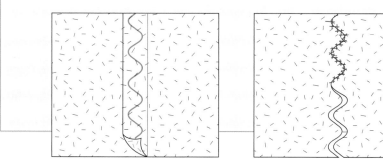

Learning the Technique

ONCE YOU'VE FINISHED YOUR QUILT TOP, it's time to layer it with the batting and backing. Then the process of hand quilting can begin. The quilting designs you choose can enhance the beauty, intricacy, or simplicity of your quilt. Knowing the hows and whys of this part of quiltmaking will assist you in making the right choices.

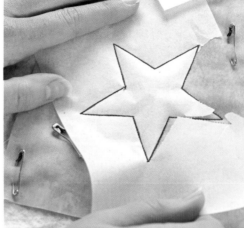

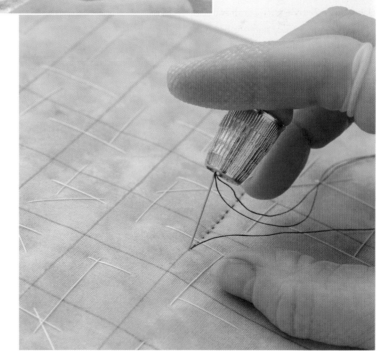

Marking the Quilt Top

Quilting designs generally are marked on a quilt top before it's layered with batting and a backing. First, select a marking method according to your project; several options follow. Then select the appropriate marking tool, keeping in mind that some marking tools are more permanent than others (see page 3).

Secure your quilt top to a large, flat work surface with tape or clips to prevent shifting. Position your quilting design in the center of your quilt top to begin. Reposition your design and quilt top as needed to mark the entire quilt center or quilt top.

Before marking your borders, see Adjusting Border Designs to Fit on page 25 for more information.

USING A TRACING METHOD

There are several tracing methods to choose from when you wish to transfer a quilting design to a quilt top. Because these methods involve placing a light source behind the layered quilting design and quilt top, tracing works best on small- to medium-size projects.

To better see how a precut stencil's design will look when it's stitched, use a pencil to lightly trace through the stencil's cutout design onto tracing paper.

Light Bulb and Glass-Top Table

1. Place a bright light beneath a glass-top table. Or pull apart a table that accommodates leaves and place a piece of glass or clear acrylic over the opening.

2. Tape the quilting design to the top of the glass. Secure the quilt top over the design, and trace the design onto the fabric.

Light Box

1. Tape the quilting design to a light box. Turn on the light source.

2. Secure the quilt top over the design, and trace the design onto the fabric.

What's a quilt sandwich? Quilters use this term to describe the quilt top, batting, and backing once they've been layered together.

Sunny Window

1. Tape the quilting design to a clean, dry window on a sunny day.

2. Tape the quilt top over the design, and trace the design onto the fabric.

USING STENCILS AND TEMPLATES

1. To transfer a quilting design using a stencil or template, place the pattern on the quilt top and secure it in place with tape or weights.

2. Mark the pattern on the fabric.

USING TEAR-AWAY PATTERNS

1. Mark the quilting design on tracing paper, tissue paper, or tear-away stabilizer. You will need to make one pattern for each time the design will be used on the quilt top.

2. Baste or pin the pattern to the quilt top. Quilt along the design lines through both the paper and the quilt.

3. Gently tear the paper patterns away from the quilt top.

USING PERFORATED PATTERNS

1. Mark the quilting design on sturdy paper. Sew over the paper's design lines with a sewing machine and an unthreaded needle (or trace the lines with a needle-pointed tracing wheel).

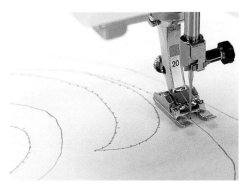

2. Secure the quilt top to a firm surface, then secure the perforated pattern to the quilt top. Go over the perforations with chalk, pounce, or stamping powder.

USING TAPE

Use quilter's tape, painter's tape, or masking tape to mark straight-line quilting designs. (See page 4 for more information on tapes.) The tape can be put in place before or after the quilt layers are sandwiched together. Reposition the tape as needed until the quilting is complete, then remove it.

To avoid a sticky residue on fabric, do not leave tape in place for extended periods of time.

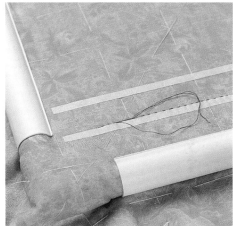

What's the difference between a stencil and a template? Both are patterns. A template is a pattern created by marking around a shape. A stencil is a pattern through which a design is transferred. Stencils have slits in the surface for you to mark through, while a template's outer edge is in the shape of its design. You can make your own stencils and templates or purchase them ready-made at a quilt shop.

Creating the "Sandwich"

THE BATTING

Once the quilt top is marked, it's time to prepare the batting.

1. Remove the batting from its packaging and spread it out on a large, flat surface to allow the folds to relax overnight. Or fluff the batting in a clothes dryer for a few minutes on an air-dry setting to remove wrinkles.

2. Trim the batting so that it's at least 3" larger on all sides than the quilt top.

THE LAYERS

Take your time layering the quilt top, batting, and backing. Being careful at this point will save frustration when quilting. It is best to assemble the layers on a large, flat surface where the entire quilt top can be spread out.

1. If the quilt backing is pieced, press all the seam allowances open. This will prevent added bulk when you are quilting.

2. Place the quilt backing wrong side up on a large, flat surface. Tape, clip, or otherwise secure the quilt backing to the work surface.

3. Center and smooth the batting atop the quilt backing. If desired, baste the batting and backing together with a single large cross-stitch in the center to prevent the layers from shifting. (This is especially important when working on a surface that's smaller than your quilt top.)

4. Center the quilt top right side up on top of the batting. To be sure that it is centered, fold it in half with the right side inside. Align the center fold of the quilt with the center of the batting, then unfold the quilt top and smooth out any wrinkles.

5. To check that you have not stretched the quilt top out of alignment during the layering process, place a square ruler in one corner. The edges of the ruler should be flush with the quilt top's edges. If the quilt is squared up, pin the border in that corner to hold it in place. Repeat in the remaining three corners. If the quilt top is not square, repeat Step 4, taking care not to stretch the quilt top.

6. Pin or baste all the layers together, beginning at the center. Being careful not to shift the layers, work toward the edges, smoothing the fabrics as you go. (Refer to the basting instructions that follow for additional information.)

THREAD BASTING

This method is most common for hand quilters because it works better in a hoop than pins.

1. With 2"-long stitches, baste the three layers together, stitching a horizontal line and a vertical line through the center of the quilt sandwich to form quadrants on the quilt top. Then baste diagonally in both directions.

2. Add basting stitches 3" to 4" apart over the entire surface of the quilt top (or follow the batting manufacturer's directions for spacing). *Note: If you'll be quilting in a hoop, use 1"- to 2"- long basting stitches spaced 1" to 2" apart. Because the hoop will be repeatedly repositioned, the shorter stitch length and closer stitches will help prevent shifting.*

SPRAY BASTING

Basting sprays are best for small projects, such as wall hangings. Follow the manufacturer's directions to adhere the layers to one another. Take care not to overspray, which can lead to gummy buildup on your needle. (See page 10 for more information on basting sprays.)

Hand Quilting

Hand quilting results in broken lines of stitches and a quilt with a soft look. Methods of hand quilting vary as much as quilters do. Adapt the techniques that follow to suit your style.

Practice pays when it comes to hand quilting. If you're new to the process, start with straight lines, then try to echo patterns. As you gain proficiency, you'll be motivated to do more, which will lead to even better results.

Small, evenly spaced stitches are the hallmark of hand quilting. A beginner should aim for evenly spaced, uniform-size stitches. Your quilting stitches will generally decrease in size as you gain experience.

HAND-QUILTING SETUP

(See pages 2–14 for more information on hand-quilting tools, supplies, and work space setup.)

Some hand quilters like to hold their quilts loosely in their laps as they stitch, a method referred to as "lap quilting."

Wooden hoops or frames are often used to hold quilt layers together for quilting, keeping them smooth and evenly taut. The layers of a quilt should be basted together before inserting them into a hoop or frame. Some quilters prefer hoops to frames because they are smaller and lighter, take up less storage space, are portable, and can be retightened as needed. The size and style you choose—whether it's a hoop you can hold in your lap, a hoop attached to a floor stand, or a large quilting frame—depend upon your personal preference and the mobility you desire. You may wish to try several types before deciding which works best for you. (See page 11 for more information.)

Hand quilters most often use a size 10 or 12 between needle and 100 percent cotton hand-quilting thread. (Hand-quilting thread differs from machine-quilting thread in that it is heavier and usually coated to help it glide more easily through the fabric.)

Be sure that you're comfortably seated, with the hoop or frame at an angle you can easily see and reach without straining your shoulders, arms, and hands. The quilt layers should be securely basted so they won't shift.

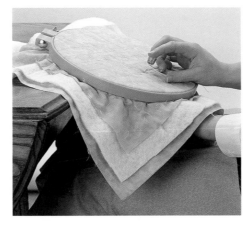

STARTING AND STOPPING HAND-QUILTING STITCHES

Stitch with an 18" length of hand-quilting thread in your needle.

You'll begin and end your stitching by burying the thread tail between the quilt's layers; this prevents knots from showing on the front or back of the quilt.

Securing Thread to Begin

1. With needle threaded, hold the thread tail over the needle, extending it about ½" above.

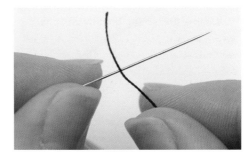

2. Holding the thread tail against the needle with one hand, use your other hand to wrap the thread around the needle clockwise two or three times.

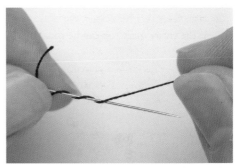

3. Pinching the thread tail and wraps with your thumb and forefinger, grasp the needle near the point; gently pull it through the thread wraps.

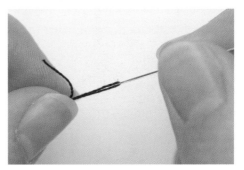

Want to work on improving your hand quilting without practicing on an actual project? Make sandwiches from scraps of fabric and batting and practice your stitching techniques on them. This is an excellent way to use your scraps and experiment with different quilting designs and stitches before trying them in a project.

4. Continue pinching the thread wraps until the thread is pulled completely through and forms a small, firm knot near the end of the thread tail. This is called a quilter's knot.

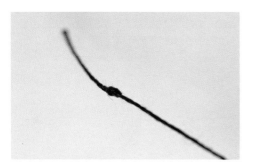

5. Insert the needle into the quilt through the quilt top and batting—but not into the backing—a few inches from where you want to quilt. Bring the needle back to the surface in position to make the first stitch.

6. Tug gently on the thread to pop the knot through the quilt top and embed it in the batting.

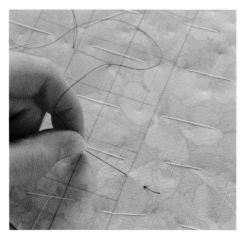

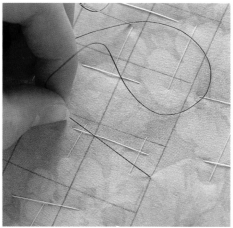

Securing Thread to End

1. Wind the thread twice around the needle close to the quilt top, as if making a French knot.

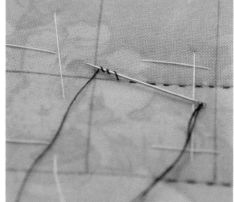

2. Holding the thread wraps next to the quilt top, run the needle tip through the quilt top and batting layers only.

3. Rock the needle tip back up, bringing the needle out ½" to 1" away from the stitching.

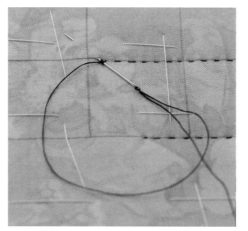

4. Tug gently on the thread to pop the knot through the quilt top and embed it in the batting.

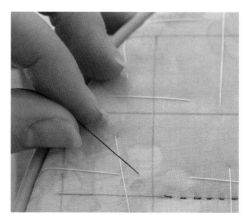

5. Holding the thread tail taut, clip the thread close to the quilt top, releasing the end to snap below the surface of the quilt top.

To decide if your quilting thread contrasts or blends the way you wish, practice your quilting designs on quilt sandwiches made from the same fabrics used in your quilt. If the color is not right, experiment with thread a shade lighter or darker.

HAND-QUILTING RUNNING STITCH

For this classic hand-quilting stitch, wear a thimble on the middle finger of your stitching hand.

1. Hold the needle between your thumb and index finger. Place your other hand under the quilt, with the tip of your index finger on the spot where the needle will come through the quilt back. With the needle angled slightly away from you, push the needle through layers until you feel the tip of the needle beneath the quilt.

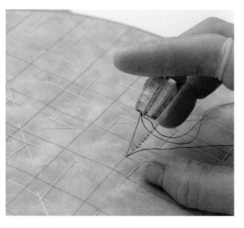

2. When you feel the needle tip, slide your finger underneath the quilt toward you, pushing up against the side of the needle to help return it to the top. At the same time, with your top hand, roll the needle away from you. Gently push the needle forward and up through the quilt layers until the amount of the needle showing is the length you want the next stitch to be.

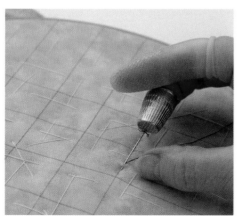

3. Lift the eye of the needle with your thimble finger, positioning your thumb just ahead of the stitching. Rock the eye of the needle upward until the needle is almost perpendicular to the quilt top and the tip is in the fabric. Push down on the needle until you feel the tip beneath the quilt again.

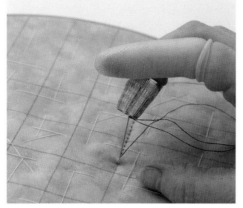

4. As in Step 2, push the needle tip with your underneath finger and roll the eye of the needle down and forward with your thimble finger to return the needle tip to the top.

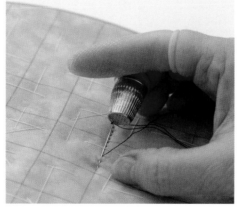

5. Repeat this rock-and-roll motion until the needle is full.

6. Pull the needle away from the quilt top until the stitches are snug.

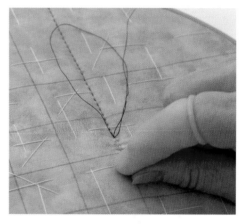

Remember that uniformity in stitch length is more important than the actual length of individual stitches.

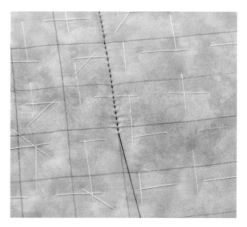

HAND-QUILTING STAB STITCH

Although it's less commonly used than the running stitch, some hand quilters prefer the stab stitch. Wear a thimble on the middle finger of both your hands.

1. Hold the needle between your thumb and index finger. Place your other hand under the quilt. Put the needle tip in the fabric with the needle straight up and down. Push the needle through layers and pull it completely through with your underneath hand.

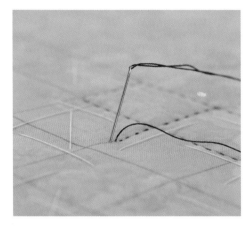

2. With the underneath hand, push the needle back through all the quilt layers to the top a one-stitch distance from where it went down; pull the needle and thread completely through all the layers with the upper hand to complete a quilting stitch.

3. Repeat this stab-and-pull-through motion, making one quilting stitch at a time.

Remember that uniformity in stitch length is more important than the actual length of individual stitches.

TRAVELING WITH THE NEEDLE

If you finish a line of hand quilting with plenty of thread still in your needle, you may want to move to another area without knotting your thread and starting again. The technique for doing so is referred to as "traveling," which is often used for continuous quilting designs, such as feathers. If the distance you need to travel is more than 1" to 2", however, it is best to knot the thread and begin again.

1. When you finish a line of stitching, run the needle point through the quilt top and batting only, moving it towards the next quilting area. If you are using a contrasting thread color that is darker than the quilt top, be sure to slide the needle deep into the batting. Bring the needle tip out about half a needle length away. Do not pull the needle all the way through unless you have reached the point where the next stitching line is to begin.

2. If you have not reached the starting point of the next stitching line, grasp the tip of the needle only. Leaving the eye of the needle between the quilt layers, pivot the needle eye toward the point where the next stitching line will begin.

3. With a thimble on your middle finger, push the tip of the needle, eye first, toward the next starting point. Bring the eye of the needle out at the starting point, pulling out the entire needle, eye first. Begin stitching where desired.

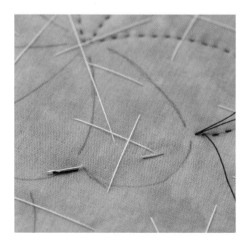

HAND-QUILTING DESIGNS

The designs that can be created with hand quilting are almost limitless. You can create straight lines of quilting stitches or intricate curves. For inspiration, see Quilt as Desired on page 24.

Tying a Quilt

Tying, or tufting, is a quick alternative to hand or machine quilting. A tie is a stitch taken through all three layers of the quilt and knotted on the quilt top surface or, occasionally, on the back of the quilt.

Tied quilts have a puffier look than those that are quilted. For extra puffiness, use a thicker than customary batting or multiple layers of batting.

Make certain the batting you select is appropriate for tying because there will be large unquilted areas between ties. (See pages 12–14 for more information on selecting a batting.)

1. Use perle cotton, sport-weight yarn, or narrow ribbon for the ties and a darner or chenille needle (see pages 6–8 for more information on needles).

Make a single running stitch through all quilt layers, beginning and ending on the quilt top and leaving a 3" tail.

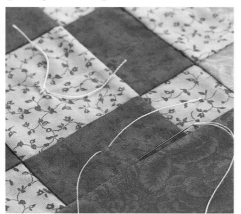

2. Make a single backstitch through the same holes and all three layers, ending on the quilt top.

3. Clip the thread, yarn, or ribbon, leaving a second 3" tail.

4. Tie the tails in a square knot (right over left, then left over right) close to the surface of the quilt.

Avoid pulling too tight and puckering the fabric.

5. Clip the thread tails as desired.

If you're assembling a quilt on a table that is smaller than the quilt backing, center the fabric on the table top so equal lengths hang down on each side like a tablecloth.

Quilt as Desired

Instructions for making a quilt generally come with detailed steps, numerous patterns, and helpful diagrams. How you should quilt the project often goes unsaid. Many quiltmakers simply quilt in the ditch or in an allover meandering pattern because they don't know what else to do.

If "quilt as desired" is your only instruction, those three words needn't leave you wondering how to proceed. Instead, look at them as an invitation to begin the next phase of completing a fabulous quilt project.

QUESTIONS TO ASK

Take some time and ask yourself the following questions. They'll help you make decisions on how to quilt your project.

Is this a quilt I hope will remain in my family for several generations?

When creating an heirloom quilt, consider quilting the project with elaborate designs and intricate details. For other projects, simple quilting designs that are easy to complete may be more appropriate.

Is this quilt going to be laundered often?

Select machine quilting for quilts that will receive lots of use.

How much time do I have to complete this quilt?

Save hand quilting for projects where you can afford to invest the time. If time is limited but you want to hand-quilt a project, select easy-to-do designs and motifs.

What's my preferred quilting method, by hand or by machine?

Just as when selecting a project, if you're excited about the process you've chosen, you'll be more likely to finish it successfully.

Whether you want to hand- or machine-quilt may also affect your choice of a quilting design, as some lend themselves better to one technique than the other. For example, if you're going to machine-quilt, a continuous line design is often the best option since there will be less starting and stopping.

Do I want my quilting stitches to be visible in the quilt top?

Save intricate, close quilting for projects that will showcase the stitching and more basic designs for those with busier fabrics and more pieces where it's likely the quilting stitches won't show.

Does this quilt have a traditional, folk art, or contemporary mood?

Sometimes the feel of a quilt will drive the quilting design. For example, a traditional quilt may call for a feathered wreath design, but a folk art quilt may look best with big stitches quilted in perle cotton.

FINDING INSPIRATION

Ideas for quilting motifs and designs don't have to be limited to the precut stencils, templates, and books of quilting designs available at your local quilt shop. Look around you for inspiration. One way to generate designs is to think about your project's theme. For example, if you're making a Christmas quilt, consider holiday-related items, such as ornaments, strings of lights, trees, holly, garland, mittens, snowflakes, reindeer, and stockings, as potential quilting motifs.

Evaluate the possibilities based on difficulty and where they might work best on your quilt. A round ornament could be stitched as a simple circle, for instance, while a reindeer would probably require a stencil. A wavy line with occasional loops could represent garland on a narrow inner border.

Another place to find a quilting design is within the quilt's fabrics. Are there motifs in one of the prints, such as oak leaves or flowers, that could work as a quilting design?

The architecture of buildings can provide numerous concepts. For instance, the exteriors of old brick buildings often provide interesting grid arrangements that can be translated into quilting patterns. Wrought-iron fences and gates might suggest beautiful scrollwork, perfect for border designs. Door arches, moldings, or pressed-tin ceilings may offer ideas for your next medallion-style quilt.

Even household items such as picture frames, jewelry, and kitchen tiles can produce quilting design ideas. The bubbles in an aquarium, for example, may suggest the perfect pattern for a goldfish quilt.

Examine both new and old quilts that you like. Ask yourself: Why do I like this quilt? What about it appeals to me? Is it the pieced or appliquéd pattern? Is it the colors? Or is it the quilting design that brings it all together?

QUILTING TERMINOLOGY

Understanding some general quilting terms will help you select a design for your next project.

Allover designs, particularly geometrics, can be stitched over an entire quilt without regard to shapes or fabrics. Allover designs can be quilted from either the top side or the backing.

Backgrounds and fillers fill in open interior spaces, such as setting squares, circles, or hearts, with stitching. You can stitch squares, diamonds, clamshells, or other small regular shapes. You also can stitch these shapes in the background outside an appliqué or quilted motif. The closely spaced lines of a filler tend to flatten the area, creating a low-relief, textured appearance.

Big, or utility, stitches require a heavier thread, such as perle cotton, and a large hand stitch. They result in a folk art appearance.

Echo quilting involves stitching multiple lines that follow the outline of an appliqué or other design element, repeating its shape. The evenly spaced quilting lines should be ¼" to ½" apart. You can use echo quilting to completely fill a background.

In the ditch means stitching just inside a seam line. The stitches disappear into the seam, which makes a patch, block, or motif stand out from its background. It's an easy method to do by machine.

Outline quilting is done ¼" from a seam line or edge of an appliqué shape, just past the extra thickness of the pressed seam allowance. If you want to quilt closer to a seam line, choose the side opposite the pressed seam allowance.

Stippling, also called allover meandering or puzzle quilting, can be stitched by hand or machine. It involves random curves, straight rows of regularly placed stitches (lined up or staggered), or random zigzags. For the best effect, stippling should be closely spaced.

BORDER DESIGNS AND BALANCE

Borders and quilt centers are usually quilted separately. While one option is to leave the border unquilted, Doing so tends to make the final project look unbalanced. That' also the result if the border quilting doesn't fit the rest of the project.

Avoid skimping on quilting in the borders; try to keep the amount of quilting equal to the rest of the quilt.

To balance your quilting designs, include the borders when you begin thinking about quilting designs for your blocks. Think about what will coordinate with or complement the quilting designs you've selected for the rest of the quilt top.

If you've selected a particular motif or design for the quilt center, is there a way to continue that same motif or a variation of the motif in the border? For example, if the blocks are quilted with a simple flower, can it be repeated in the border, maybe by adding a connecting vine-and-leaf pattern? If you are crosshatching the blocks, can you crosshatch through the border as well?

As you select your quilting designs, evaluate the fabric used in the border. Is it a solid or a subtle print that will really show off a quilting design? Or is the fabric so busy it will hide any type of quilting?

If you have a solid inner border and a print outer border, you may want to quilt a recognizable pattern in the solid border, where it will show up better, and then crosshatch or stipple the busier fabric.

AUDITIONING DESIGNS

Once you have an idea for a border quilting design, it's best to create a paper template or tracing paper overlay to see how the design will fit in the length of your borders and how it will turn the corners. Use a temporary quilting pencil or marker to draw it on your quilt top.

Always test the pencil or marker on scraps of the fabrics used in the quilt top before marking on the actual top. (See Marking the Quilt Top, which begins on page 16, for more information.)

ADJUSTING BORDER DESIGNS TO FIT

There is no single formula for success in adjusting border designs to fit a quilt. Because of the variety of factors involved—border width and length, quilting design width and repeat—the ways to adjust a border design are numerous.

An important consideration as you adjust the design is that it is best for all sides and corners to match. The most challenging method is to adjust the length of a continuous design. However, there are options other than adjusting a border design's width and length.

Extending the Center Design

If an overall design, such as crosshatching or stippling, was used on the quilt center, consider extending it onto the borders as well.

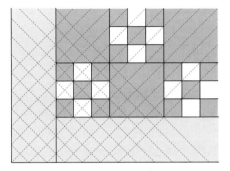

Meandering Vine Design

Meander a vine design along each border. When you reach the corners, be sure to turn the design in an identical manner, creating mirror images in opposite corners.

Repeated Block Design

Repeat a block design used in the quilt center in the border (or choose a different design), evenly spacing the design along the length. Pay particular attention to the direction of the motifs. You may wish to point them all in one direction if the motif has a definite top and bottom. Or you can point all the designs toward or away from the quilt center.

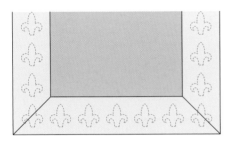

Combining Elements

If you choose a rhythmic or wavy design, such as swags or feathers, but the motifs don't fit, consider combining them with a block design at the midpoint of each border.

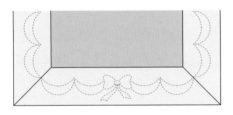

Adjusting the Length of the Design

Adjusting a continuous line design takes the most time and effort of any adjustment but, when completed, results in a design which appears to seamlessly circle the entire quilt. The instructions that follow are for modifying a stencil design. Drawing the design first on paper (shelf liner or freezer paper) will prevent you from incorrectly marking your quilt top.

Though the steps for adjusting border designs are generally the same, how you choose to add or take out extra length so that the design fits is unique to each project.

As a rule, it's best not to modify a design at the corners. Instead, adjust the design somewhere near, but not at, the midpoint.

1. Cut two lengths of paper, one equal in width and length to the quilt's finished side borders and one equal in width and length to the top/bottom borders. Do not include the seam allowances. (If your quilt is square, one strip will do.) Label the strips and mark the center of each.

2. Trace the stencil's corner design on the ends of each strip. Use the registration marks on the stencil to make sure your design is properly aligned on the paper border.

3. Align the center registration mark on the stencil with the midpoint marked on the border. Beginning from this point, slide the stencil between the midpoint and corner to figure how many repetitions of the design will fit. The alterations will likely be different for the side and top/bottom borders.

If the amount of design adjustment is small, you may be able to adjust a bit of length in one motif without noticeably altering the design. *Note: If the amount to be added or reduced is too great, the design will be distorted, calling attention to the motif that was squeezed or stretched to fit.*

If the amount is significant, you will need to add or delete a part of several motifs to make the adjustment. When doing so, keep in mind the overall shape of the design and use the stencil as much as possible to trace the design on the paper.

4. Once you're pleased with the paper patterns, transfer the modified design to the quilt top. (See Marking the Quilt Top on page 16.)

Choose a border design that fills the border's width well, keeping in mind you don't want the quilting to go too near the seam allowance or you'll risk covering it with the binding.

Having trouble basting a large quilt without the layers shifting? Often the problem is not having a large enough work space to lay the entire quilt flat. Working on the floor is less than desirable and hard on your back. If work space is at a premium in your home, see if there's basting space at your local quilt shop, community center, or church. The large tables often found in these places can be pushed together to make a surface that's easy to work around without having to adjust the quilt.

Gallery of Quilting Designs

STYMIED AT THE THOUGHT OF PLANNING A QUILTING DESIGN for your pieced quilt top? Don't be! The ideas and examples that follow are loaded with creative solutions to delight and inspire you. Some of the samples featured are quilted by hand, others by machine. Simply choose and adapt your favorites to make your finished piece an exciting, personal expression of your needlework skills.

1 Nautical quilting designs abound in this sailboat quilt. Hand-stitched waves fill the white border, and a swirling pattern adds motion to the water and sky.

2 The center section of this quilt is machine-stitched with an interlocking orange-peel design. The leaves in the border, joined with deeply arched vines, are half the orange-peel design.

3 A puffy wool batting made machine-quilting this project an excellent choice. This serpentine stitch is easy enough for beginners.

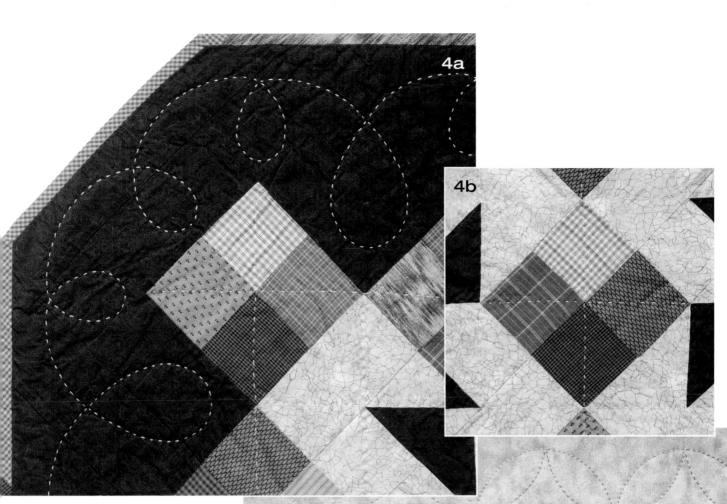

4 Arches connect simple teardrop shapes (4a) in this border. Using contrasting perle cotton on the dark flannel produced a country look. A quick, simple hand-quilting technique, aptly named "big stitch" (4a and 4b), creates the primitive, folk art look on the border and the Four-Patch block (4b).

5 This border's lovely curved quilting, done with a heavier specialty thread and a sewing machine, complements the quilt center's elaborate embroidery.

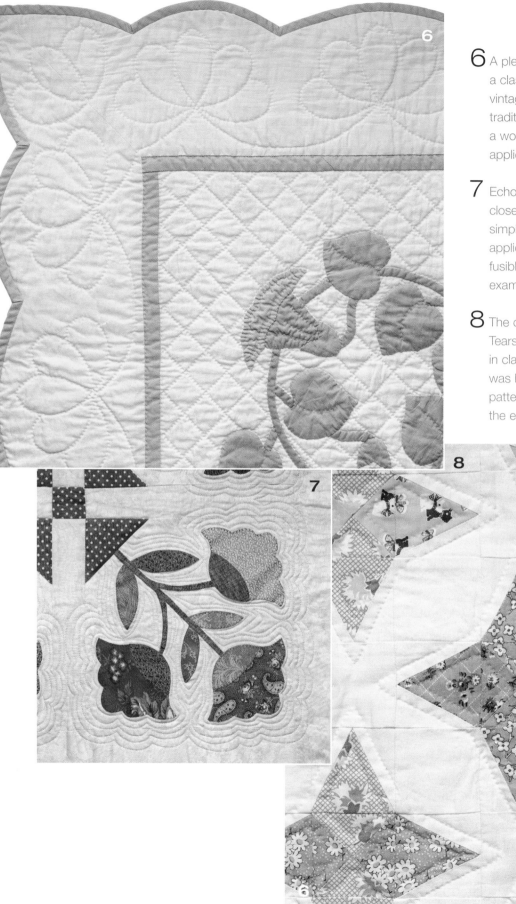

6 A pleasant scalloped edge frames a classic looped border in this vintage hand-quilted piece. The traditional crosshatching creates a wonderful backdrop for the appliquéd blocks.

7 Echo quilting can be done with closely spaced concentric lines that simply follow the contours of the appliqué pieces, as was done in this fusible-appliqué project. This example is stitched by machine.

8 The outline quilting of Job's Tears, a traditional pattern done here in classic 1930s reproduction prints, was hand-stitched ¼" inside each pattern piece, as well as ¼" from the edge of each four-point star.

9   Stippling provides texture and interest behind a pattern, such as this appliqué shape. This project was stippled by machine.

10   Kaleidoscope, a traditional block, naturally gives the illusion of movement. To accentuate the spin in the design, the maker machine-quilted circles in each block.

11   Viewed from the back, this allover machine-quilted design reveals free-form loops and feathers. On the front, this type of allover quilting blends sampler blocks of many hues.

12 Machine-quilted logs and machine-quilted smoke curling from the chimney were natural choices for this Log Cabin block.

13 A patchwork dinosaur marches across a background of machine-quilted pebbles.

14 To complement this quilt's starry-night theme, the quiltmaker machine-stitched fireworks, or chrysanthemum, shapes in the inner border.

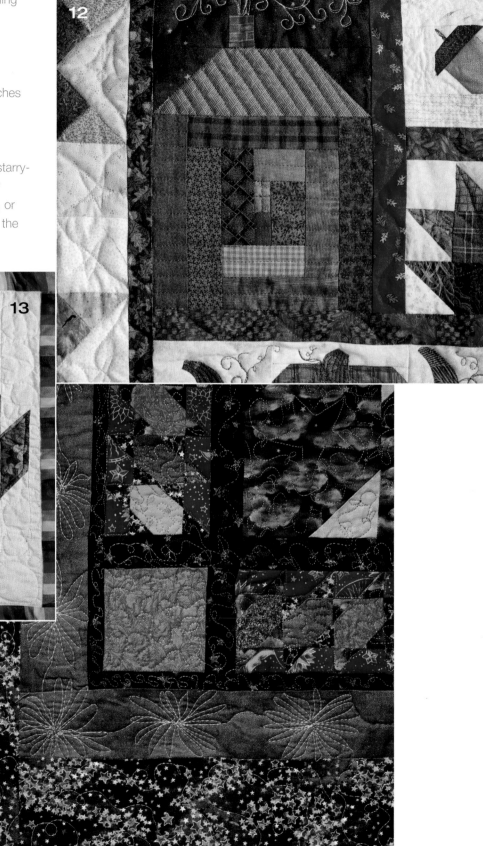

15 Random big stitches, using contrasting perle cotton on a cream-color background, add specks of color for a creative filler.

16 The lines outlining this angel's wings are faux stitches. They were drawn on with a permanent-ink pen.

17 The designer of this colorful hand-quilted design chose a swirling spiral pattern for each setting square to offset the angular piecing.

18 The layers of this Nine-Patch quilt are tied together with perle cotton for a simple, unfussy feel.

19 Carefully placed, machine-quilted concentric circles add interest to these simple star blocks.

20 This hand-quilted design, inspired by Mother Nature, is fittingly called a spiderweb pattern.

21 Maple Leaf blocks in autumn colors made the designer think of a rainy fall day, so she machine-quilted overlapping circles to create the illusion of leaves floating on water.

22 The metallic thread used here to stitch in the ditch makes the machine quilting a design element. Often, however, in-the-ditch quilting is nearly invisible as the thread disappears into the seams.

23 Cookie cutters were used as patterns for the hand-quilted stars scattered around this project's plaid border.

A Pair of Wholecloth Projects

YOU MAY HAVE A PIECED TOP THAT'S READY FOR QUILTING and have already decided to make it your first hand-quilting project. If so, consider this duo for their quilting pattern ideas. However, if you're starting from scratch, these small, wholecloth projects (made from a single piece of fabric) will give you plenty of opportunity to practice and perfect your hand-quilting technique.

FLORAL
Medallion

If you're inspired to try a wholecloth quilt,
designer Pepper Cory's tabletop-size project
is the perfect place to start.

Photographs by Craig Anderson and Perry Struse

Materials

30" square of solid white for
  quilt top
¼ yard of solid teal for binding
30" square of backing fabric
30" square of quilt batting
Quilting/between needles
Quilting thread: white and contrasting
Basting thread: white

Finished quilt: 24½" square

Quantities specified for 44/45"-wide,
100% cotton fabrics.

Mark the Design

The patterns are at *right* and on *pages 39–41.*

1. Before placing the design on the quilt top,
mark the top with as many registration lines
as you need. Use a rolling chalk wheel with
dust-away chalk to designate the center of the
30"-square solid white quilt top. Use long
acrylic rulers and squares to help you delineate
specific areas, such as an X from corner to

corner or lines that designate a border
and its corners. Some quilters like to
crease registration lines by folding the
quilt top and pressing the lines. Consider
your climate before depending on creased
lines; in humid regions pressed marks
may disappear before you have time to
draw your designs.

Mark a line 2" from each edge
of the quilt top to allow for seam
allowances and trimming after the
quilting is complete.

2. Referring to the Quilting
Placement Diagram, *page 40,*
place the Floral Medallion Center
Design on a light table, and secure it in
place. Place the marked solid white quilt top
on the quilting design, aligning it over your
placement lines and centering the design.
Using a quilter's pencil, transfer the design
to the quilt top.

Rotate the quilt top on the pattern, then
transfer the remaining three points on the
center circle.

3. In the same manner, transfer the Floral
Medallion Border Design to each corner of the
quilt top, transferring first the right-hand
design of each corner, then reversing the pattern
to trace the left-hand design of each corner.

Complete the Quilt

From solid teal, cut:
● 3—2½×42" binding strips

1. With wrong sides together, layer the
marked solid white square and the 30"
backing with the batting sandwiched in
between; baste the layers together.

Floral Medallion
Border Design Quilting Pattern
(⅛ of design)

Match the dots and the boxes on
the pattern sections, *opposite* and
at left, to complete the pattern.

Floral Medallion
Quilting Placement Diagram

Match the dots and boxes on the pattern sections, *below* and *opposite,* to complete the pattern.

2. Quilt the marked design, beginning from the center. The fancy designs on this project were hand-quilted with pale green thread and the plain quilting (crosshatching) with white thread. (The photograph on *page 38* shows the reverse side of the quilt.)

Make "erase as you quilt" your motto. After each quilting session, gently erase the marks behind your just-completed stitches. This way, you'll never be stuck with a grubby, must-be-washed quilt when you're done. If marks are in pencil, a pencil eraser works fine. A gray fabric eraser, available at quilt stores,

also is good. Don't use a hard pink eraser, as it contains grit and can leave nubby bits of rubber in your quilting stitches.

3. Trim the quilt to 25" square, including the seam allowances.

4. Use the solid teal 2½×42" strips to bind the quilt according to the instructions on page 45.

Floral Medallion
Center Design Quilting Pattern

FROM
Little Acorns

Together, trapunto and hand quilting can create impressive results. Here, project designer Mary Stori carefully explains every step of trapunto, which involves outlining a design, then stuffing it so it stands out in high relief.

Photographs by Perry Struse and Steve Struse

History of Trapunto

Wholecloth solid-color quilts have been viewed with great admiration since early colonial days. Worked with intricate, finely hand-stitched patterns, these designs displayed a stitcher's mastery and often took years to complete.

Sometimes the quilting motifs were stuffed to create a raised surface, while the backgrounds were closely stipple-quilted to flatten and texturize the fabric and accentuate the high relief of the designs. This technique of padding a design from behind came to be called, among other things, trapunto.

Because this style of quiltmaking looks so impressive, it's considered difficult to do. Quiltmaker Mary Stori disagrees. "It's a little time-consuming," Mary says, "but difficult, no." She says the biggest challenge of trapunto is learning how to stuff the motifs without cutting into the quilt's backing fabric.

Mary believes all quiltmakers can become proficient at trapunto. The steps that follow for this project contain her insights to help even the most inexperienced quilter tackle this technique. Once mastered, trapunto can be incorporated into plain setting blocks for pieced quilts, featured in borders, or used as the centerpiece of a larger wholecloth quilt.

Trapunto projects can be hand- or machine-quilted. Mary chooses to hand-quilt hers because, she says, "hand-quilting is my favorite part of the quiltmaking process."

The Design

Because the quilting motif generally dictates the theme of a trapunto project, Mary selects the quilting design first, then she chooses her fabric colors. Many of her quilting motifs are based on things from nature. "Nature doesn't create perfectly shaped leaves, flowers, or vines, and it's for that very reason I like these subjects," Mary says. "Since nature isn't perfect, I don't have to be either. Therefore, there's more room for the inevitable 'oops' as the design is drawn, traced, and even quilted."

What does matter is the design's scale and spacing. For example, it's more interesting to have some leaves that are large and some that are small, because it creates depth. Pay particular attention to narrow areas, such as vines and stems, to be sure there is enough room—at least $\frac{1}{4}$"—to allow cording to be worked in between the quilting lines. Also, study the pattern's arrangement to ascertain that there's enough space around each motif to allow for the all-important background quilting. Design elements placed too close together will not be distinguishable.

The Supplies
Fabric

Wholecloth quilts are most effective when a solid-color fabric and matching thread are used. The pattern in a print fabric will camouflage the stitching and a high-contrast thread will overpower subtle designs, so the texture you desire will not be as evident.

For your main fabric, select a good-quality, medium-weight, woven 100 percent cotton. "I love to use hand-dyed fabrics because they add richness to the piece," Mary says, "but I stay away from the mottled ones."

Underlining

Mary uses yarn and fiberfill to stuff the motifs. To avoid cutting into the backing fabric to insert the stuffing material, she bastes an additional layer of fabric, an underlining, to the wrong side of a marked quilt top before the quilt sandwich has been created. This underlining holds the stuffing material in place once a cavity is created by stitching around the motifs. Mary prefers to use 100 percent cotton muslin for underlining because the weave is firm enough to keep the raised work on the top of the quilt rather than allowing it to push into the back.

Stuffing Supplies

To stuff narrow channels, Mary uses acrylic rug yarn in a color that matches the fabric, if possible, and a No. 16 yarn darning needle. Larger motifs can be filled more effectively with polyester fiberfill; do not use quilt batting as it's too dense. A chopstick, stiletto, or tool designed for stuffing works well to push the stuffing into the motifs. She works on one motif at a time, which allows her to add just the right amount of stuffing material and avoid distorting the fabric's surface.

Batting

For small wall hangings Mary uses a thin polyester batting. This thin batting works especially well because it hand-quilts easily, and it doesn't beard or add bulk to the quilt. It also has good stability. Plus, it doesn't require prewashing and won't shrink when laundered.

Thread

The color of the thread used for quilting is more important than its fiber content. The thread and fabric color must match as closely as possible. For this project Mary used a specialty thread. However, if you're a trapunto beginner and are quilting by hand, you might want to avoid specialty threads because of their tendency to break and fray.

Materials

2—18" squares of solid rust for quilt top and backing
1—18" square of muslin
1—18" square of thin polyester batting
¼ yard of black print for binding
Polyester fiberfill for stuffing
6 yards of rust-color acrylic rug yarn
Quilting/between needles
No. 16 yarn darning needle
Quilting thread to match the fabric
White basting thread
Black permanent fine-point pen
White tracing paper
Masking tape
Small sharp embroidery scissors
Light box (optional)

Finished quilt top: 14" square

Quantities specified for 44/45"-wide, 100% cotton fabrics. All measurements include a ¼" seam allowance.

Fabric Preparation

1. Use a black permanent-ink pen to trace the Quilting Design, *pages 46–47*, onto white paper. Use a nonpermanent marking tool to mark a 14½" square onto the center of a solid rust 18" square. With the aid of a light source (a light box or window), trace the quilting motif inside the marked rust square (see Photo 1); fill out the design with an extra leaf, if desired. ***Note:*** *If you use a stencil as a quilting motif in a future project, you don't need to first trace it onto white paper.*

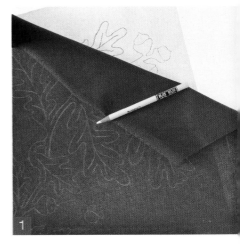

2. Baste the muslin to the wrong side of the marked rust square. To prevent shifting while basting, tape the corners of the muslin, then the marked top, to a work surface. Using a smaller than normal basting stitch, sew just inside the marked lines of the quilting motifs (see Photo 2). The veins on the leaves can be sewn slightly to the right or left of the marked lines. For better visibility, use white thread. ***Note:*** *This process creates the cavities that will be stuffed.*

3. Turn the fabric layers so the muslin side is up. With small sharp embroidery scissors, carefully trim away the muslin underlining, except what's behind the design motifs, retaining a ¼" seam allowance (see Photo 3). Some intersections of leaves and branches may not allow enough space to provide sufficient seam allowances if cut, so leave those areas untrimmed. This step reduces the quilt's bulk, making it easier to hand-quilt. Machine quilters can skip this trimming step if they prefer.

Pad the Design

1. To pad the design motifs, work from the back side of the quilt top. Use yarn to "cord" narrow channels, small motifs, or little portions of large motifs. Begin by inserting a darning needle threaded with about 12" to 16" of rug yarn through the muslin underlining; run it between the muslin and the basted rust square (see Photo 4). Leave a

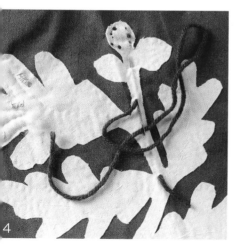

2" tail at the beginning to avoid a gap in the filling in case you pull too hard on the yarn as you move it along. Manipulate the needle through the channel or motif, gathering as much fabric as you can. Bring the needle out of the muslin when it becomes difficult to proceed, and pull the yarn through the channel or motif. Reenter in the exit hole, and continue until the channel or motif is filled with yarn. Trim the ends of the yarn close to the fabric. Some wider channels or motifs may require two or more passes with yarn. It's best to fill with single strands of yarn; double strands have a tendency to twist together and appear as lumps on the quilt top.

2. Use fiberfill to stuff the larger design motifs. Still working from the back, use small embroidery scissors to cut a small slit in the muslin underlining in the center of the motif, such as a leaf, or a section of a motif. Be careful not to cut into the basted rust square.

Working on a flat surface, insert small bits of fiberfill into the cavity with the aid of a blunt stuffing tool (see Photo 5). Stuff only tiny bits at a time until the design is lightly but evenly stuffed. Avoid overfilling, which may cause the fabric surrounding the design to pucker. Turn the project over from time to time to check for distortion (see Photo 6). If necessary, adjust the amount of fiberfill. Once a motif is stuffed, use a needle and thread to whipstitch the opening in the muslin underlining closed.

Complete the Quilt

From black print, cut:
- 2—2¼×42" strips

1. Secure the corners of the remaining solid rust 18" square to a table with small pieces of masking tape in preparation for basting the quilt layers. Cover with the batting square, and position the trapunto quilt top over the batting, right side up. Generously baste the three layers together with stitches about 2" apart.

2. Begin quilting by outline-stitching around all the motifs on the marked lines; quilt additional design lines in the leaves. Remove the small basting stitches from the motifs (the outline quilting now takes over their job).

3. Finish quilting the project with a desired background quilting pattern, such as a ¼" diagonal grid. Mary hand-quilted a meandering stipple pattern in her quilt.

4. Trim the quilt to 14½" square, including the seam allowances.

5. Use the black print 2¼×42" strips to bind the quilt according to the instructions that follow.

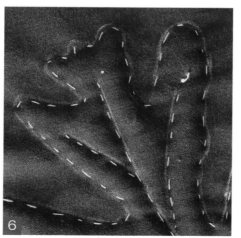

From Little Acorns
Quilting Design

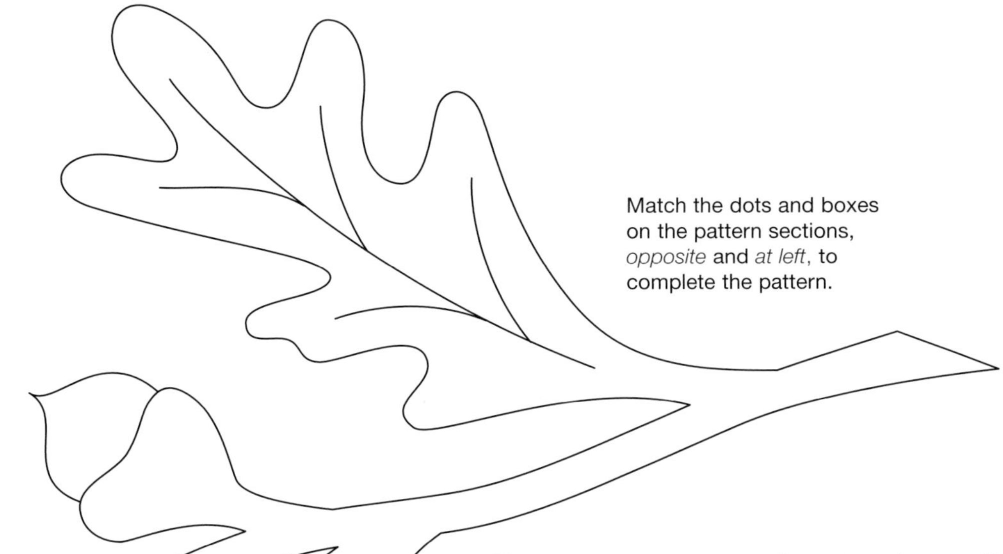

Match the dots and boxes on the pattern sections, *opposite* and *at left*, to complete the pattern.

7. Beginning in the center of one side, place the binding strip against the right side of the quilt top, aligning the binding strip's raw edges with the quilt top's raw edge (see Diagram 4). Sew through all layers, stopping ¼" from the corner. Backstitch, then clip the threads. Remove the quilt from under the sewing-machine presser foot. Fold the binding strip upward (see Diagram 5), creating a diagonal fold, and finger-press.

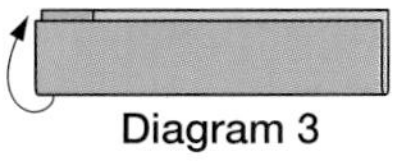

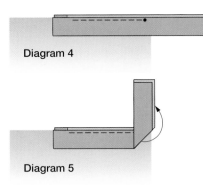

Diagram 4

Diagram 5

6. Join the strips with diagonal seams to make one continuous binding strip (see Diagram 1). Trim the excess fabric, leaving ¼" seam allowances. Press seam allowances open. Then, with the wrong sides together, fold under 1" at one end of the binding strip (see Diagram 2); press. Fold the strip in half lengthwise (see Diagram 3); press.

8. Holding the diagonal fold in place with your finger, bring the binding strip down in line with the next edge, making a horizontal fold that aligns with the top edge of the quilt (see Diagram 6).

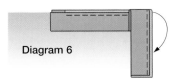

Diagram 6

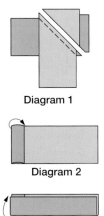

Diagram 1

Diagram 2

Diagram 3

9. Start sewing again at the top of the horizontal fold, stitching through all layers. Sew around the quilt, turning each corner in the same manner. When you return to the starting point, lap the binding strip inside the beginning fold (see Diagram 7). Finish sewing to the starting point (see Diagram 8). Trim the batting and backing fabric even with the quilt top edges.

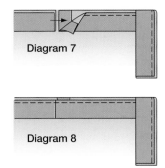

Diagram 7

Diagram 8

10. Turn the binding over the edge of the quilt to the back. Hand-stitch the binding to the backing fabric, making sure to cover any machine stitching.

11. To make mitered corners on the back, hand-stitch the binding up to a corner; fold a miter in the binding. Take a stitch or two in the fold to secure it. Then stitch the binding in place up to the next corner. Finish each corner in the same manner.

Better Homes and Gardens®
Creative Collection™

Editorial Director
Gayle Goodson Butler

Editor in Chief Deborah Gore Ohrn

Executive Editor Karman Wittry Hotchkiss

Managing Editor Kathleen Armentrout

Contributing Editorial Manager Heidi Palkovic

Contributing Design Director Tracy DeVenney

Contributing Editor	Laura Holtorf Collins
Contributing Designer	Kim Hopkins
Copy Chief	Mary Heaton
Contributing Copy Editor	Mary Helen Schiltz
Proofreader	Joleen F. Ross
Administrative Assistant	Lori Eggers

Executive Vice President
Bob Mate

Publishing Group President
Jack Griffin

Chairman and CEO William T. Kerr
President and COO Stephen M. Lacy

In Memoriam
E. T. Meredith III (1933–2003)

ISBN 1-60140-052-7